[DEVIANT REFLECTIONS]

By

**Bill C. Castengera**

# Other Books By Bill C. Castengera:

## Shift!

The Apocalypse, teleportation, social vices, and an alcoholic God. This satirical Sci-Fi is a must-get laugh riot!

"Satirical fiction at the wackiest angle concievable."

## Half Full

Changing the way we think and know ourselves changes our reality

## In Less Than 60 Seconds: Ultra-Short Flash Fiction

Ultra-short flash fiction for those that love to read but don't have a lot of time. It's a great bathroom book!

# The Paparazzi Made Me Do It

The paparazzi flashes burn spots in my vision. They all want a piece. The really good ones say things to antagonize me, to get a rise, so they can sell the footage to TMZ. If I lose control, if I lash out, maybe an attorney will pick up the case, maybe ratings go up on the shows that replay my outburst. But for now, they can't. Because there's no mob, no paparazzi, no flash. No one points at me in awe because *Oh my God, I'm actually, like, right here.* No one is star struck. I'm not somebody.

I tell myself, I'd be that guy, that one exception. Charismatic. Always willing to stop and talk for a bit to the press, the fans, whoever. I would have infinite patience. I'm not some fucking pre-Madonna. I would show them my humility. They would see that I'm a really down-to-earth guy, not some entitled shithead.

"I don't deserve this," I'd say.

But somewhere, sometime between year five and six during my rocket to fame, I would start to develop a stand-offish attitude. I told myself I'd be cool and calm, but they don't leave you the fuck alone.

"I'm shaking the urine off the tip of my penis right now, maybe I can answer your questions when I've finished this. Just this bit here, the shaking of my penis. No. Wait. I'll answer. Yes. I'll answer right now, but you need to know the whole time we talk, I'll be holding my junk. You're okay with that? Ok. Yes. I guess you are."

I will start to see them as vultures, and I'll try to avoid them. The patience I expected to have would have worn off years ago, but no, these assholes would have me on the edge and I would lose the ability to fake it. After they wear me down, I just become an asshole, and that's all they ever wanted. It's a story. For the tabloids. Now it's sellable, a complete package, because nobody gives a shit about a nice guy. They mold you into who they want you to be and you simply can't resist. They force you to be an asshole. See that? It's not my fault. These guys are professional asshole creators.

But not right now. Right now it's quiet and I can go to a grocery store and people barely even look at me. I'm a ghost. A ninja. I disappear without hiding. Right now the ocean of my potential fame is calm. That's why I write. The face of a writer is blank. It is unknown and it will stay unknown. I know what they look like, but I wouldn't recognize John Grisham or Michael Crichton if they were standing next to me in the line for tickets to the Tri-County Gumball Chewing Contest. Even if one of them weren't dead. Writers are faceless. They are supposed to be. Stephen King obviously fucked up. He lost his anonymity.

Anyway. All I'm saying to you now is that the paparazzi create the shitheads the stars become. It's not their fault. See what they did to Lindsey Lohan? The guy that did that was a paparazzi black belt.

# Default Condition: Misery

The default condition for humans is misery. We thrive in it. We are capable of amazing things because of it. Our desire to break free from it has fueled the industrial and technological age. Cars were invented to escape it. Television was realized to pull us from the grasp of misery's dull drum, and communications of today have wiped away the vastness of distance. But here we are. Still miserable.

It is a virtual hell. There is no hell on Earth because hell *is* Earth. Better yet…we have created a perpetual hell in our minds. Humanity is insatiable. Satisfaction is fleeting. Happiness is fleeting. It can be sustained only long enough to want more of it. Happiness is a hallucinogenic, a drug. The more we get, the more we want. We'll go to any length to get it. It wears us down. And we continue our misery. The dope man wants more and more from us for ever-reducing amounts of happiness. He knows we're hooked.

Human productivity is a reducing factor. The more we produce to ease our misery, the lazier we become. There will be an event horizon, a time where laziness and productivity will coexist on an even plane. Eventually laziness will win the day, and the fall of humanity will be apparent. We're getting close already. End times, the apocalypse, whatever. Predictions have been made. Grab your shotguns and food rations, we're turning the corner directly into it. That underground bunker I once laughed at is taunting me now. It's fine. Fuck the bunker. My plan is to go out in a blaze of miserable glory. I'll fire shots into the air and laugh wildly as the cannibals approach.

# Fuel.

I use malice to fuel my workout at the gym. It seems to work better than happiness. I'm all for using happiness as a tool to accomplish something, but you have to pick the right tool for the job. So, anger. Frustration. Those emotions are great workout fuel. And even though it seems like a negative thing, I like to think about how I'm using negative emotions to affect a positive outcome.

I'm laying with my back flat against the workout bench, perfecting my grip on the bar, preparing to lift it off the rack and push out eight to twelve reps of heavy-ass iron plates. I'm thinking of the massive printer jam at work, thinking about how I opened the door it told me to open to clear the jam, but there's no jam and how I'm letting this inanimate electronic piece of shit dictate my actions, but also how it's leading me astray and it just can't fucking fix because I'm on a freaking time crunch and it's the goddamn perfect time to fucking break and….

One.

The car at the stoplight in front of me doesn't go when the light turns green. It's no problem, I'm pretty patient. I wait for a moment. I can see the driver is on the phone, not looking up. The car behind me honks to get things going. It was a respectful honk, just one staccato, a light touch of the horn. The lady in the car in front of me glances into her rear view mirror and we lock eyes. No problem. She raises her hand and gives me the middle finger as though I was the one who honked and was being an impatient asshole, and now I want to run up to her car and grab the back of her head and smash her face so hard into her steering wheel that it deploys her airbag…

Two. A bead of sweat trickles down my forehead.

My computer screen flickers gently as I type. I'm working on budgets in the office. The guy at the desk next to me is working on his computer as well. Not sure what he's working on, but if I listen to him commentate long enough I can figure it out. He clicks his tongue, he mumbles to himself about having to delete this email and send out that email. He talks quietly about opening a spreadsheet and moving cell A1 to cell F9. I don't suffer from misophonia, but can't this guy shut his stupid mouth long enough for me to concentrate? He clicks his tongue while he thinks and I actually prefer the tongue-clicking to the mumbled play-by-play. Also, I'm about to snap. Michael Douglas's character in the movie *Falling Down* would hesitate to approach me. I want to stretch out a roll of duct tape and wrap his whole fucking head in it while screaming, "SHUT THE FUCK UP!!!" so loud that it causes his eardrums to rupture and begin to bleed…

Three.

I stand in line. Doesn't matter where. The two young girls in front of me are talking to one another. They are children. Maybe fourteen or fifteen. They actually use the term OMG in speech. I sort-of accept it. They keep talking. One of them LOLs. She *actually* says "LOL." This I cannot accept, but also literally between every word in her sentence she uses the word "like," and I want to claw my own ears off my head because not only is it a snapshot of the youth of today, it's the death of a language, the massacre of human intellect and it's who we are going to leave this country to. I want to Mike Tyson my own ears and lament the death of intellect…

Four. My arms shake from the weight of the lift, muscle failure is coming, desired fatigue setting in.

I have a pocket in my shirt on my left breast. Every shirt I wear at work has this pocket. It rests neatly next to my tie. It's professional. I'm not sure if the pocket is really supposed to be a functioning part of business attire or if it is a decorative asset to remember the past, to pay a sort of *homage* to a time when it really was a functional standard. Either way, I use it as a functional asset. I keep things in it like pens or paper clips, whatever. When I lean over far enough, the contents of this pocket are dumped. Stupidly, I pick up all of the contents and replace them back into the very pocket that betrayed me in the first place. Not even a minute passes by before, for one reason or another, I again lean over too far, spilling the same contents onto the floor. Fuck this pocket. Fuck it for being in a convenient location to hold shit. It seduces me into using it and it repeatedly betrays my trust. I want to punish this pocket by yanking it right off my shirt. Teach it a lesson. Stop fucking with me, pocket…

Five. I almost can't lift it all the way up this time. I have no spotter. If I can't lift it all the way up to re-rack the bar, it could lay on my chest indefinitely and trap me. Someone will have to come over and rescue me. So I rack the bar. I'm pissed that last week I was able to get out ten reps with this same weight. I can't figure out the variables. What did I eat? Did I get enough sleep? My only consolation is that I can use this failure to fuel my workout next week.

I'm not crazy. I am utilizing crazy thoughts to create positive outcomes. I secretly wonder if the justification is enough or if it will send me on a spiral down a rabbit hole of actual assault. Time will tell, time will tell…

# Narcissistically Disproportionate

Three decades down, pining away on the fourth and I still can't believe it. Pop culture damaged me. Magazine covers ruined any realistic perception of women I ought to have. I don't blame them, though. They're trying to sell fucking magazines, not pander to obese girls hiding in the closet clutching a box of cookies and a Hersey's syrup bottle. Self-confidence is a dream. Most of us have our arms stretched out, arching the knuckles on our fingers to near-hyper extension, trying to float on top of the water. Too bad we lack the required webbing in between those pudgy digits. You'd think we'd float by sheer buoyancy. But no. We sink. Staying afloat is an act of willful determination. So it's difficult.

You've seen them. They make it look easy. Confidence sweats out of them like delicious honey. They ooze. The only reason I want to be near them is to maybe catch some of the ricochet. The honey ricochet. That's what we want from them. But they work for it too, the sneaky bastards. Spray tans and fad diets, all around. Starving themselves until they satisfy their need to see the outline of their rib cage. Each rib is like a tree ring indicating levels of beauty, levels of healthy superiority. Malnourished is the new healthy. Those kids in Somalia own a country of potential pageant winners. The horn of Africa, they call it. But they can't afford the entry fee. Plus, lack of domestic crops is an unfair advantage. They'd throw off the whole handicap if we let them play. Let them be bony and beautiful from afar. That way, our fat American bitches can at least have a chance.

Aim for high cheekbones, sunken in. The sinew and neck muscles almost rip through their skin since it's so tight. They wish the calories in that blueberry muffin they ate last week would go straight to their lips. Fat lips is the new sexy. I should go into business and punch these idiots in their mouths. I might even go pro bono and throw in a freebie from time to time. They leave the really talented caricature artists at the carnival nothing to draw. The work has already been completed by a Beverly Hills plastic surgeon named Julian. At least he takes off his Yakama during the procedure. It's not a surgery anymore, it's a procedure. Surgery gives us the impression of the correction of some health ailment. Procedures are exactly the opposite. They are creating the health ailment which will need to be surgically corrected at a later date.

All of this to fill the narcissistic need to look the way the media wants them to. To sell fucking magazines.

# I Quit.

Today I told my boss I'm quitting.  There is a certain
resolve one must maintain to pull off a professional
resignation.  Every molecule in my body wanted to slam him with
reasons why it's his fault and his alone.  But it's not just his fault,
and the things that need to change are things so far out of his
wheelhouse, it would be pointless to even bring up.  Silence.  He's
not local and he's only around about once a month to tell me what I
need to improve.  A quick white-glove inspection, a demoralizing
beat-down, and then he's gone again.  So I'm on the phone with
him, in the seconds after I say it and now the silence is stretching
out longer and longer until it starts to get awkward.  It's like an
auditory staring contest.  I already knew I was going to lose because
the silence on the phone was so weird and long that I wasn't sure
we were still connected.

As I took a breath in to say something, he lost whatever
advantage the silence gave him.  He finally broke it.  "I don't accept
your resignation."  Aw, I'm blushing!  He likes me!  He really
really likes me!  Who knew?  It's either that or he doesn't want to
be bothered to find a replacement.  Dammit.  Yes, that has to be
it.  But I know I'm good at what I do.  It's like I'm in an abusive
relationship.  All I really want is love and nurturing, and all I ever
get is a kick in the stomach.  The stomach.  Don't leave any visible
bruising because if I suddenly decide to scream foul, no one
believes me.  I'm battered.  And I try harder for that approval, one
step beyond what I was doing before.  He always got what he
wanted from me.  And I pretended not to see what he was doing and
I took the beatings like a champ.  My smile never faded.  On the
inside, though, I was exhausted.

Andy Dufrense taught me to patiently bide my time.  This
job was Shawshank.  I took the beatings and now my escape was
apparent.  My boss was stunned that I was even unhappy.  He was
obviously out of touch.  But I will be free soon.  I thanked him for

his guidance, mentoring, and leadership. All lies. I don't burn bridges, I prop them up.

He tried a few last ditch efforts to save me. Offered things that I politely refused. A transfer, a lateral move, a step down with no pay decrease. HR has an exit interview scheduled with me later that will be useless to them. I'm doctoring the data. I won't tell them the truth of why I'm leaving. You may call it cowardice, but I call it quiet dignity. There is no reason to trash the place despite my desire to. It's up to the others to save themselves. I escaped on my own, no Underground Railroad, no pre-paved path to freedom. I forged my own path and they can do it too. The burden has been lifted and I'm hopeful for the new challenges I might face somewhere else.

# Smart Confusion

I'm smart. That's not a gratuitous plug, it's a fact. Arrogance doesn't even enter the equation. Supposing that I'm not only a good judge of character, but also give myself extra credit points for a high level of self-worth, does this mean I'm better than anyone? I don't think so. Being smart is a damaging disadvantage. It is responsible for creating the social outcast you now have before you. Self-inflation, transparent vanity, and how I believe myself to be the king of everything, if I haven't lost you yet, is not what this is about. It's about dumbing down. Everything everywhere. Lower your standards so that you might be able to interact with your peers. First of all, self, don't tell me what to do. And second, these are not my peers…are they?

I twist my face like a tornado spinning on a curly fry. It's hectic and greasy. Is it delicious? I really can't tell. I'm confused. While confusion is the opposite of the intelligence I just claimed, I have to admit it. I'm confused. I'm confused by popular television shows and how they can entertain more than a microscopic segment of the population. I'm confused by the show Swamp People. I'm confused by the affinity for Honey Boo Boo. I don't understand how a terminal cancer-laden high school teacher that decides to cook crystal meth is even remotely entertaining. Is this what we have become?

Maybe I'm just being pretentious. Maybe I'm not smart at all. It's very possible that I have a severe psychosis. My perception of reality is that it shouldn't be the way it is. But it is this way, which means that I am wrong.

I watch people. I see people have full conversations. But they're not *saying* anything. We have lost a personal touch. Was it the red pill or the blue pill that opened Neo's eyes? I don't remember, but I feel awake amidst a sleeping population buried in their cell phones. I was talking to a girl earlier today and she never even looked at me. The glowing square of light in her hand held much more intrinsic value than actual human interaction. We cannot multi-task. But we think we can. She thought she was easily pulling off texting while interacting with me. I don't know if she ever looked up, but if she did, she would have seen me walking away. Not worth it. And it's not her fault, it's mine. I am flawed because I think it should be some other way.

Dumb down, ok? Conform. Stop rocking this little canoe we confiscated from the Native Americans. If you don't fall in line they'll try to brainwash you into it. Pop culture will do it for them. All you have to do is sit there and take it all in. Listen to the messages. You don't even have to believe them at first, you just have to listen. When you finally look up, your unique identity has vanished, replaced by the collective, a hive of millions. You can't really expect to grow from it. Proclivity to individually produce has popped out of existence and you have become a slave without ever realizing it.

If you can wake up, if you can intelligently pull yourself up and celebrate individualism, you will finally see my eyes, because I was here, patiently waiting for you to see me.

# Everything Changes – A Moment Of Clarity

A few last days to button it all up. Then a change of pace. I'm not a fan of change, not really, but I can tolerate it. It's a good thing, too, because change is all there really ever is. A few beers last night, a triangle slab of tuna, and a club of yellow squash pushed me through the epiphany. It occurred to me that epiphanies often strike me when my cheeks are loaded up like a squirrel's, the sudden realization of constant change forcing me to stop mid-chew.

I always feel like I eat like royalty, but not in the proper sense, more like a Dark Ages noble, where I use my hands and chicken grease slithers down my chin, but I don't care to wipe it before it drips. I imagine the sounds of it, like I'm breathing through my mouth in between giant bites of a horse sized turkey leg. Meat only, because I'm not savvy enough to farm–or have people farm for me. I don't know. I consciously have to slow it down so I don't elicit stares. I never savor my food. Eating is a necessary function, not a pleasurable experience. It's more like a wild animal gnawing at its meal quickly before another animal can take it away from me. It's a base instinct. But I have refined the ability to hide that edge. So I slow it down. Way down. And I've begun to incorporate vegetables, very unlike the medieval nobility.

So anyway, I say that to say this: during my dinner last night, when I had the epiphany of constant change, I realized that despite slowing it way down, I still stuff my stupid face to capacity. When I stopped in mid-chew, my cheeks were actually stretching, causing the outside corners of my eyes to pull. What the fuck? Immediately I stopped giving a shit about the idea of constant change and replaced it with the new epiphany that I'm a disgusting pig. However I'd thought I'd managed to curb that wild animal inside me, well, I hadn't. I rationalized. Sometimes I'm hungry and I have to eat fast…but the excuse just wasn't doing it for me. I'm an animal. A foul, unrefined, wretched animal with not a shred of social grace.

I talk with my mouth full. I chew loudly. Food flies from my mouth. I mean big chunks. Chunks of food that might be a full fucking meal for a native tribe that is facing famine. They could stretch that chunk for weeks. In my ultimate defense, and hopefully, this is mere perception, maybe I'm not as bad as I'm describing here. But my mind deals in extremes and so this is how I perceive myself.

To tie this all in as best I can, all I'm saying is that I had an epiphany of a world that is in constant flux, a world that rapidly changes. In tandem with this realization, I also consciously decided that I need to change how I eat. It can't be healthy. Most likely I am shocking my body by inundating it with food at an alarming rate. The digestive process just can't catch up. It's not the sort of realization that will leave a lasting mark on the world like I thought it was going to be when I first came to it, but it is the type of thing that I probably should take a long hard look at.

# Beer And Landscaping

Drink some beer, mow the lawn, earbuds in, music loud, and focused. That's my plan today. People look almost affronted when I tell them I love to do yard work. It's not very pleasant. The Florida heat is unforgiving. It makes even the easiest outdoor project feel like a marathon through molasses. That's what the beer is for.

At first, it's an instant refresher. It's cool, lowering my internal body temperature. But that's not the goal. Not really. A few in and coupled with acceptance of the fact that I'm going to sweat–that I actually resign myself to sweat–and just let it happen, the fun really gets a grip on me when my liver's efficiency fails to catch up to all the beer I've ingested. It's dangerous, like I'm walking across a plank above starving alligators Indiana Jones style. The heat dehydrates, the beer dehydrates. The coffee I drank when I woke up is a diuretic. It dehydrates. Heat exhaustion could occur. I'm a dangerous man, living on the edge of insanity, because fuck you, nature.

There is something about a freshly mowed lawn, near-perfect edging, and highly manicured hedges that float my boat. It's an ego thing, maybe. It's something no one but me really gives a shit about, but it's a personal, internal sort of achievement. It's alone time with hard work. I listen to music, get lost in the activity, and sweat all of the toxins out of my body…admittedly while putting in new toxins…but not only that. It's *productive.*

I remember a time when I was deep into the routine of my yard work, deep into the consumption of alcohol, and drenched with sweat. I have a decent sized oak tree in my front yard, and to mow the lawn around the tree, I had to duck under the branches that were hanging down. I decided to cut down a few branches to make any and all future yard-mowings crouch free. Fast forward about thirty minutes to when my wife pulled into the driveway, and I can only imagine her view.

I had climbed the tree and was sitting on one of the thicker branches, a beer in one hand and a chainsaw in the other. I was stretching down to cut a lower branch. She honked the horn to get my attention since the music was loud in my ears, the whir of the chainsaw adding to the auditory onslaught. I turned off the chainsaw and took one earbud out of my ear, leaving the other in to hear what she was trying to tell me from below.

"I think you should come down from there," she said. She said it calmly, but the look in hers eyes told a different story. It was clear that she believed I was taking my own life into my hands. Maybe she was right, but the alcohol consumption had boosted my confidence and at that moment I saw nothing wrong with the fact that I was ten feet in the air with a beer and a chainsaw. Luckily, my instincts took over and the many years of marriage had trained me to comply. I agreed to come down.

The yard looked damn good though.

# Life Lessons I Might Or Might Not Learn

It's sunny outside and all I want to do right now is curl up in the fetal position in a darkened room and take a glorious nap. I'm fatigued. My mind wanders like a hobo. I'm trying to figure out why I'm so exhausted right now. It could be any number of reasons.

Drinking too much last night really should top the list, but no vomiting means that I didn't get anywhere near my threshold. The two mile bike ride this morning? Maybe. Right now, I'm sitting in a freshly banded deck chair by a pool that burns my nostrils with the smell of chlorine. I like that smell. It gives me the impression of a chemical clean. I like it because I feel that the only way something can get clean enough is by using abrasive, toxic chemicals. It's counter-intuitive. The spray of the nearby kiddie water park is misting my phone as I write this, and though it's a cooling relief, I'm a little annoyed by it. Annoyed while sitting in a tropical paradise by a clean pool. Of all the things to be annoyed about…

I might be tired because of the fact that yesterday I finally got back in the gym for the first time in two weeks. Or because I mowed the shit out of my yard yesterday afterwards. That's when the drinking began.

I made chicken, pepper, and sausage kabobs on the grill afterwards. Fatigued, but at least I feel like a productive mother fucker. I'm basking in being human, in making other people feel like they can't accomplish enough by comparison. But this pace will eventually cause me to hit the hurdle and skin my knee. It'll probably be worse than that. I'll knock it over, skin my chin and palms, break an arm. Then productivity will be out the window.

There are kids at this pool. Little rat bastards. I like kids as a general rule, except when they act like spoiled little shitheads. This kids is spraying people on the deck with his water shooter. He does not belong to the people he's spraying and he's laughing his bratty little ass off. Where the fuck are his parents? I think if he sprays me, I will probably push him down. Usually my tolerance level is a little higher but I'm too tired to allow myself to be bullied by a ten year old. Also, I have no self-respect. Not enough, anyway, to not push a kid down if he deserves it. Could be a good life lesson that he could carry with him for the rest of his life. Don't be a shithead. Lesson learned. And if I push him down, maybe his dad might see it and teach me that same lesson....That way, we all leave the pool having learned some valuable piece of information about respecting others.

# Cheerleaders. I hate them.

Cheerleaders. Not those bitches with the pony tails and the tiny duel-tone skirts. I'm talking about normal people that like things too much. Advocates. Yes. Advocates. They champion things. They believe shit. They believe *in* things. They are positive and cheerful and super out-going. That's why I hate them.

These people are confident in their own skin. Too confident. I feel insignificant next their stupid bubbly personalities. They know everyone. They hug people hello and goodbye. And I'm there, and since I'm not willing to give someone a hello fuck, I'm standoffish.

It's not even that, really. It's the fact that these people push ideas. They are the propaganda pushers, the religious wackos, the campaign presidents, the PTA moms, and the field trip chaperones. While they try to come off as selfless, actually they are exactly the opposite.

They want people to like them. Desperately. I am the antithesis, the bizarro cheerleader. I spew hate, but at least I do it mostly internally. Mostly because I'm a coward. No, maybe it's not that. Maybe it's because I wish I had that ability to be über-supportive–or at least give the impression of it…but I don't and I can't, because I am too inside my own mind. Constantly. So in order to counterbalance these titans of team spirit, I project the opposite. It somehow makes me feel better about myself, which ultimately just amplifies the severity of my introversion.

I'll be the old man that yells at the kids to get off my lawn. The old codger that still thinks he can kick the ass of someone half his age. I'll pick up a penny I see on the sidewalk, and glance around out of the corner of my eye to see if anyone is watching. So fuck the youngsters. Fuck the millennials of tomorrow. The millennial millennials. I cringe away from supporting a good cause. I am not a cheerleader, not an advocate. I am simply the precursor to the old man that hugs young girls just little too long and tries to negotiate the price of a matinee movie ticket.

There must be a place for the future old bastard I will become. But even if there's not, I'll forge the path so that the anti-cheerleaders can have a cheerleader of their own. I can be the irony, the hypocritical exception to my own rule, an advocate for non-advocacy. And then I will hate myself even more than I already do.

# Not A Bystander

I'm not a good bystander.  I'm not good at just standing somewhere like an idiot and watching things happen around me.  I need to *interact* with my environment.  Not people.  The environment.  Let's be very clear about this.  I do *not* want to interact with people on a personal level.  I can handle small doses, but I can't keep up the "being normal" act for any extended length of time.

My mind is twisted in angles that would make a contortionist's forehead bead with nervous sweat.  I don't mean twisted in the metaphorical sense.  I'm not saying that I'm sinister or dark or anything like that.  I'm just saying I don't fit in with the traditional idea of societal normality.  I'm weird.  There are twists and turns my mind takes that are way too far off the beaten fucking path.  People can't live in my world for very long, as I can't live in theirs.  We can all visit for short stints, but we both wear out our welcome pretty quickly.

I'm not the guy behind the security tape, behind the person getting interviewed on the news.  I can't be that guy.  He's the bystander, the witness to what happened.  He's the guy that was eating at the bistro when the Hulk smashed through the fucking wall.  He didn't get hurt, but he watched a bunch of bricks fall on some woman's head, her children with their ice cream cones in mid-lick, suddenly orphaned.  He's the guy that doesn't matter.  The guy that sent a head shot in and got the part–as an extra.  He is "construction worker #3".

Have some self-respect, man!  Be more than a bystander.  Be more than a witness to events.  But, shit, don't *participate*.  Participation is dangerous.  You've got to find that sweet spot, that limbo between bystander and participant.  That's where I typically fall.  There's a seat reserved for me there.  In the 'weirdo' section.  Not many people have exclusivity to it.  Not many people even want it. Everyone is weird, everyone has some small quirk that makes them a little off. That's fine. But I'm not that. I have some small quirk that makes me normal. It is fleeting and rarely seen. It's the Loch Ness Monster. Bigfoot. There have been sightings but the rarity of those sightings turns it into an urban legend. And when people look at me, they are just not sure that normality is even there at all.

# The Gym. My 'One Weird Trick' Revealed!!

The gym. I go because I have low self-esteem and a poor body image. In odd counterpoint, I also go because I'm incredibly vain. It's a conundrum, a paradox. They simply can't be simultaneously true. But here we are. It's a weird pair. Someone, somewhere once used the word "athletic" to describe my physique. Yesterday, a girl told me I was looking "buff." These descriptions are ridiculous, for the record. These people have never seen me naked, never had the supreme displeasure of witnessing how my fat belly curls over my belt. I'm a disgusting fat pig. But also, I am a good-looking sonofabitch!

I do bust my ass at the gym, though. I work hard. I lift very heavy weights. I go all out. Also, I am there for less than an hour each time and I only go two days a week. I've been doing this for about five years. The results have been slow, but there have been results. The only reason I have sustained this rigorous two day a week schedule is to justify the insane amounts of beer I ingest.

So here's how I work this: I work five days a week. I have two days off. Do the math, it works. I don't go to the gym on a day that I work. Also, I don't drink on a day that I work. On my day off, say, around 8:00 AM, I wake up, eat a light meal, and then hit the gym. I focus all of my energy and effort on getting an amazing workout. The one thing that allows me to get through the pain of this amazing workout is the knowledge that it will not last longer than an hour. I can't think about the future step or I will lose all focus. The future step? After my exhausting workout, I binge drink for the rest of the day. I stop drinking around 7:00 or 8:00 o'clock.

That's how I spend every day off. It really can't be healthy, but surprisingly, I have managed to pack on some muscle over the few years that I've been doing this. Think I can commercialize this as "one weird trick?" Probably not. I can't condone this sort of irresponsible behavior. So the less-than-an-hour workout justifies the binge drinking and against what should be right and holy with the universe, I look like a decently muscled Cross-fitter.

The above description, I must say here, is only accurate when you add clothes to the equation. I look fit——in clothes. Take them off and the whole dynamic changes. Babies see me and cry, women choke back tears of vomit. Tears of vomit. Yes, you read that right, because it is sad and disgusting all at the same time. I am not a wild and majestic mustang galloping in the Colorado foothills. I'm more like a buffalo, sucking in his stomach to pass for a mustang. It's way more obvious when the clothes come off. Luckily, most of my interactions occur while I'm fully clothed. Let them think I'm the mustang.

To sum it up: work out insanely hard for less than an hour. Binge drink for the rest of the day. Two days a week. For five years. Simple! That's my "one weird trick." Hope this helps! Also, as a side note, I recommend against this.

That is all.

# I'm Going "Flowers For Algernon" Mode

Like Charlie in *Flowers for Algernon*, going from knowing everything to knowing nothing is just the worst. Granted, Charlie went from knowing nothing, to knowing everything, then back to knowing nothing. The middle is where the action is, anyway. If you ever get a chance to read it, you should do it. It's a short story by Daniel Keyes, so it won't eat up very much time.

Basically it's about Charlie, who is mentally challenged, and Algernon, a laboratory mouse. Scientists, by virtue of being scientists are able to give the mouse a drug and it suddenly gets very smart. Sort of like that movie *Limitless* or *Lucy.* Good movies, both, by the way. Obviously, without FDA approval, they also give Charlie this same drug and so he starts getting smarter. The mouse is on treatment a few days ahead of Charlie so any side effect that happens to the mouse, Charlie experiences too. It's a long explanation to get to my point, but read the short story. It's a fucking classic.

Anyway…

This story is sort of like my life right now except it starts in the middle because I'm not–I keep telling myself, anyway–mentally challenged to begin with. I went from knowing everything to knowing nothing. That's tough, man. The reason for this, if you've been following my blog posts, or at least haphazardly following them and just happened to read the blog in particular that describes how I quit my job, is because now I've started a new job.

God! I was a virtual wizard at my old job. I knew the systems, solved the problems, and was a mentor for less experienced, albeit bright-eyed and naïve, colleagues. I was the answer man. From that, I basically became Charlie at the end of *Flowers For Algernon.* Or at the beginning. Take your pick. But definitely not from the middle.

So I started a new job, and I'm learning new systems and methods. I am the last person someone would want to ask for help. It is humbling, but it's sort of what I wanted. At my old job, I was just going through the motions. I was stagnant and bored. I wanted new challenges, to learn new things. I'm getting it, but I'm wondering now if my decision was worth the social humiliation of being viewed as the company's special needs case. I think its okay. I think its okay, because it's expected. At some point, though, I'm going to need to put up or shut up. I will have to prove to people that the non-FDA-approved drug is working and I'm getting smarter. Perhaps I'm starting to feel a little performance anxiety.

I'm going to be in charge of 30+ people, who all currently know more than me. Know what's worse than having to train your manager? Fucking nothing. The guy is getting paid double or triple your salary and you're teaching him how to do his job. Okay. I figured it out. I know what's worse. It's worse *being* that manager that is getting trained by his subordinates.

Here's the bottom line. I need to accelerate my meteoric rise to the top. Finish the novel, sell more of my first. Write full time and end this pain. The 2 people that will end up reading this blog post will be able to say they've followed my story from the beginning. When I was Charlie. Or a lab mouse at the end of the story, even though I'd really like to think it's just the beginning. Until it all unfolds, we simply can't know.

# Anger Management For The Masses

Group anger management courses. That's what society needs. Government mandated, required by law, anger management classes. The world is filled with people that have no control over their emotions. We are like infants except we have learned a language and gained functional motor skills. Both great accomplishments, but then we use those gifts to verbally berate other people and physically accost each other.

For the record, I am for less government control, but I just can't believe that people will try to rectify this on their own. We need to be forced into submission, to be bent toward harmony. And if not harmony, then at the very least, we need to be taught how to quench our desire to throat-punch someone.

Society is off the tracks. Friction doesn't exist here. By all accounts, once the train derails, it should make contact with the ground and eventually screech to a halt. But the train slides on, against the asphalt, sparks flying into the air and never stopping. It careens out of control and doesn't slow down. It takes out buildings and it clips cars. It is relentless.

Link it to a driver's license as a prerequisite. I don't know. Something. We have lost order. We don't respect our fellow humans. We are selfish. We can't seem to muster up the courage to consider different viewpoints.

I hate everything that society has become, and ultimately that's why I want to collectively throat-punch the whole world's population all at once.

# The Fifth Circle Of Hell. Dante Wrote It For Me

Forever stuck in the fifth circle of hell, a free ride on the river Styx. Dante should have given me my very own ring, but he didn't know me. It would have at least evened out the total rings to ten. Satan deserves the tenth ring, not the ninth…

So anyway, the fifth ring is for people who lived cruel, vindictive, and hateful lives. Maybe I'm being too hard on myself, but also, maybe I'll see the whole world's population there when I get there.

I'm beat today. I just spent the whole day at work, stayed late, and worked fast and accurate. I cut my lunch short. I was productive. I didn't even do it to impress my boss. I did it to make someone else tell my boss that he should be impressed with my work ethic. It's not going to work, though. It never does. Because people can't see past their own needs and ambitions. Why say something good about someone when that person isn't there to appreciate them for the good things they just said?

That's why I'll be in the fifth ring. I don't even mind that much. I'm more put off by the rings full of idiots I'll have to trudge through to get to my spot. Whatever. If there were a ring of hell for complainers, I would be the leader of that ring.

Crazy thing about it is that I don't outwardly project a negative attitude. People tell me I'm positive. Guess I could be one of those <u>cheerleaders</u>. On the outside, at least. Internally, I'm as cynical as they come.

I think both of my ankles are broken. Like Vito just crushed one with a sledge hammer for owing him some money and not making good on it. "You've got a nudder one," he'll say. Then he'll threaten to break the good one in two days and turn me loose onto the city streets. Only I didn't make good, and now I have two worthless stumps at the end of each leg. I need Dr. Scholl to take a charity case. My feet need some serious support. Prescription strength support, not this over-the-counter shit. I need potency.

When did I get so old that I complain about how bad my feet hurt after a long day at work? Today. Today I became that old. It's all downhill from here, folks. Lucky for me I'm still absurdly attractive.

I swear I remember that there was a ring of hell for vanity...but maybe not. I'll look it up and not update anyone. Sorry, just being honest. Maybe that was from the movie *Se7en*. Morgan Freedman. Watch it if you like sinning, and Verbal Kent. Also if you like Tyler Durden. I'm getting way off-track, here, and no one understands any of my references anyway so I'll pick up a more coherent line of thought next time.

I sort of promise.

# Technology Can't Wipe Out The Caveman

The traditional way to kill an octopus is by biting its head and crushing its brain with your teeth. People still do it. It's sort of a rite of passage, a way to pay homage to our fore bearers. It's a tradition. And it's gross.

Technological advancement can't hide the fact that we live in a giant swamp. We contend with natural forces like snakes, mosquitos, hurricanes and floods. We get eaten by sharks, attacked by bears, and die from the heat and cold. We are still cavemen. Cavemen with iPads.

Our bodies produce pheromones. We sweat like animals, and we poop. We are biological, a product of the muddy crust on which we crawl. We still have our caves, but now our caves are custom. They're designed. Instead of drawings on the wall, we hang pictures, the need to adorn our walls deeply rooted within us.

All I'm saying is that we are no different now than the hunters and gatherers that came before us. We have not advanced. We have produced an illusion of advancement. But things are the same. We are the same.

I know, I know. We deserve at least a little credit for scientific achievements. We have cured disease, traveled to the moon, and learned how to communicate across the globe in mere seconds. I get it. I do. But we are still cavemen—with gadgets. Our minds have drastically outstripped our biology.

I'm not sure what I'm expecting, what sort of biological, evolutionary awakening I think we ought to have had by now. I mean, shouldn't we be telepathic by now? At the very least? What kind of advanced civilization can't communicate telepathically? Shouldn't we be able to shoot lasers from our eyes or mentally manipulate gravity?  Something?  Instead, we eat cow meat for dinner and bird eggs for breakfast.  It's crazy.

We are violent.  We are selfish.  We are controlled by our own base instincts and desires and I guess when I think about it that way, I just feel that humanity is closer to those cavemen than the transcended entity for which it gives itself credit.  How can we feel like advanced beings when we use our technological prowess to play candy crush?

So until the evolutionary switch gets flipped, I guess we'll still be biting octopus heads.  It's not even necessary, but how, then, would anyone know that testosterone runs through my veins like blood?  I'm not scared.  I'll bite the head off a squirrel.  A cat.  A moose.  I'll caveman the fuck out.

# Time Travel:
# Rewinding Time

Run the tape on rewind. Watch it unfold backwards. Watch it refold. It's not even accurate to say rewind anymore. Nothing winds, therefore nothing rewinds. That era is over. Doc Brown could fire up the DeLorean, but I suddenly remember—that story is fiction.

We can't grab the past, all we can see are the reflections of influence the past plays on the present. It's development. The present is watered-down past and I'm not sure I would want to go back anyway. Sometimes the change we think we would make would redesign the whole landscape. The butterfly effect. Maybe you take your chances. Maybe the difference would be better, but maybe not. Then go back and change the change. Happiness is a figment of our imaginations. It's fleeting.

So here we are, H.G. Wells, relaying the story to us in first-person, like its real and we get confused. High-falutin' chatter amidst cigar smoke and brandy snifters. The boys' club is in full swing, the gentlemen discussing the possibility—the probability— of time travel. Theoretical physics, particle physics, string theory, faster-than-light travel. Einstein shakes his head so violently they have to sedate him. I imagine Kepler leaning down to Einstein as they're strapping him into the old-school straight jacket, stains of unknown origin yellowing the front of it, buckles rusty from age. So anyway, Kepler leans down to him and whispers gently into Einstein's ear, his breath heavy and hot, reeking of freshly swished brandy and he says, "It will happen, old boy. Your legacy will be lost." Einstein convulses in a panic, but the muzzle gets clipped into place at that moment and he gets hauled off.

Reality is a confusing place. It's a place where things that are conceivable could actually happen. Like in a dream. We can figure it out. We can make the dreams reality. At what point will we have nothing left to dream about? When we've completed the works we've dreamed up, when there is nothing left for our imaginations to fantasize about, from where, then, will the advancement come?

Sir Isaac Newton once said, "Identifying the existence of gravity is much like fucking whores." I'm not sure what it means, exactly. Also he never said that. But the point is this: we desire knowledge. The pursuit of knowledge can be confused with pleasure. There are people that hedonistically pursue science, like a guilty pleasure. They are insatiable, and as long as those people are out there, we will continue to turn dreams into reality. We will crush the ideas of those that broke ground before us, and they will be taken off in disgrace, as the new age of scientists replace them.

Rewind time back. It will be possible. All we need is a little time…

# The Secret Agent Inside

The Jeopardy song plays in my head, like a decision must be made and time is running out. I'm a secret agent, with a company issued jet-pack. One that has been perfected and doesn't burn my legs off. But for some reason, they need collateral from me before they allow me to borrow it. So I give up my car keys for a short aerial jaunt. Small price to pay, right? For a freaking jet-pack?

So anyway, the point I'm trying to make, albeit very poorly, is that I feel like a secret agent. I just got off track on the jet-pack deal, mostly because it's an extremely seductive idea. A secret agent, with the sunglasses and explosive chewing gum and all. I am two people. I could have ventured down the schizophrenic path, but secret agent seems way cooler. And not quite as daft. At any rate, I am living two lives. One life, they see. The other, I hide behind the first.

My mind explodes with random ridiculous thoughts and images, all stitched together with a normalizing thread. It holds everything in. For some reason, people won't understand. My mind out paces people. I'm not saying I'm smarter than people, I'm just saying that my mind stays active. It's exhausting. I can't carry a normal conversation with people because I'm playing chess. I'm three steps ahead and I'm already where I think we're heading. The travel time it takes to get somewhere is an annoyance to me. I just want to *be* there. The scenic route winds so much it makes me nauseous. I answer questions people haven't asked yet. I'm not psychic, I'm impatient.

So I slow it down. It's a self-inflicted sedation. I'm an anesthesiologist. The medical review board refuses to give me a license though. They have deemed that just because I fantasize about self-sedation, it also somehow means I shouldn't be allowed to physically practice knocking random mother fuckers out with prescription strength drugs. Through an IV. They think they know everything. Public safety is an illusion. All it takes is one rogue anesthesiologist to implode the whole system, and pseudo-Kevorkian wanna-bes will pop up all over the place. They're here now, but the shadows they practice in are a little too dark for detection. The shadows are metaphorical and they're hidden in plain sight. That's the best way to hide.

So this brings me full circle. My personal secret agent hides. In plain sight. The sunglasses at night are the giveaway, though. The only good thing about it is that in the darkness, it's so hard to see through the sunglasses, he can't see a goddamned thing to make any sort of impact on anything.

# King George Washington

A little different this go 'round.  It seems appropriate, given the time of year here in the states for a little bit of reflection as to why people spend hundreds of dollars on explosives every first week of July.

Fifty-six treasonous signatures adorn the parchment of the Declaration of Independence.  John Hancock sprawled his across the bottom in less than subtle defiance, and I imagine the large swoops of his signature, the *audacity* of them, made the others feel a little better about gracing that parchment with their own marks.

Here's a quote from it that pretty much sums up the whole document:

*"...Governments are instituted among Men, deriving their just powers from the consent of the governed, that whenever any Form of Government becomes destructive of these ends, it is the Right of the People to alter or to abolish it..."*

Basically it is saying that we're allowed to alter or abolish our own government if it does things we don't consent to.  That's why we hold elections.  We, the *governed,* are in charge of the government.  People forget that, I think.

But also, it was a statement of separation from British rule.  The preamble is the part most people remember and quote...*We hold these truths to be self-evident*...Yada Yada...but the real meat is in the Indictment section, where it lists separately each "injury" against the American people perpetrated by the then British king, George III.  Basically it's a list of complaints, which is why it's right up my alley.  I enjoy a good list of grievances.

So anyway, these ornery bastards were probably sitting at the pub one night, sauced up, faces numb from the near-poisonous moonshine, talking about how King George III fucked them in the ass again, and one of them probably stood up and said, "You know what? This is bullshit. I'm done."

That night he went home and called up (okay, so maybe he pony-expressed them?) leaders of the thirteen existing colonies one by one and most of them said, "Fuck this, I'm done too…but only if I can get…." And the first earmark was born. Pennsylvania was the main hold out, but eventually it came around and everyone was onboard.

It was the first step to the birth of the country in which I currently reside. It was the fornication, the conception. And our forefathers forgot the protection. I think they used sheep intestines back then since latex wouldn't be invented until 1920. But that's another story…

John Adams was obviously a fan of blowing shit up. Before the Declaration of Independence was even signed, he supposedly imagined that fireworks would be a part of the festivities. Here's a little *real* history for you: On July 3, 1776, he wrote to Abigail Adams, his wife, that the occasion should be commemorated "with Pomp and Parade, with Shews, Games, Sports, Guns, Bells, Bonfires and Illuminations from one End of this Continent to the other from this Time forward forever more." Forever more? What amount of self-importance must one feel to expect people to do something forever more, just because he said to?

"Sounds good," we said. And we comply. Every year, we are honoring the wish of John Adams, and we light this bitch up.

I'd like to think that at least some percentage of our current population fully understands the cause we have to celebrate. It's not about freedom to do whatever we want whenever we want. It's about the freedom that we have, as a people on this particular swath of land, to hold to the rules and laws *we* decided to create. It is the freedom and obligation to abolish a government that becomes corrupt and stops listening to the people who govern it. We are all owners in this.

After reluctantly serving a second term, George Washington, a colonial-era badass, refused to run for a third, establishing the tradition of a maximum of two terms for a president. It was solidified by Thomas Jefferson and James Madison. Georgie-boy could have stayed in power but he didn't. That is not something to be taken lightly. Men of less integrity, hungry for power, would have stayed in office, crippling America before it could get truly started. Thank God these men understood that the office belonged to the people, not to a single individual. Otherwise, it could have been King Washington.

So now you know. And now you can light up the night sky on July 4th with purpose—forever more.

# Wake Up

Please forgive me…I'm a little introspective today…

"I'm only connected for seconds, minutes a day, sometimes. And suddenly, you go, 'Holy cow, I've been asleep for two days. I've been doing things, but I'm just out.' If I see someone who's out cold on their feet, I'm going to try to wake that person up. It's what I'd want someone to do for me. Wake me the hell up and come back to the planet." —Bill Murray, from a 2014 interview with Rolling Stone.

Leave the grind to the less creative. But I still have to play their game. I still have to function inside of the rules of what society says is normal. I guess I don't have to, but then I'll end up pick-pocketing people on the train. Probably in the dining car. I'll wear a three-piece suit, and glasses, with a pocket watch in my left vest pocket. They wouldn't even know what hit them. I'd be gone before they knew they got taken. Too bad…it's just a dream. My nerves would get the best of me, sweat beads on my forehead, shaking hands, the endorphin rush would make me talk just a little too fast. I'd be suspicious. But, shit, I'd be well dressed. That part, I could pull off.

I can fake functionality, fake normality. It's a cheat that makes people believe I'm in control, confident, and successful at what I do. When their heads are turned, I'm sneaking pieces off the game board for the advantage. Pushing my piece a little closer to the finish line, and when they turn back around, they play on without a clue. In that, my nerves are steel. No shaking hands, no stuttering, nothing. I justify it by telling myself it's different than putting my hands in someone's pockets. I justify it by telling myself it's not theft, that my moral compass stays intact. But it's just as sneaky, just as deceptive, and my moral compass is laying in shards of glass and metal. It broke years ago. I'm not sure if it ever worked at all. True north is not an indication of where I am, it's an obstacle to where I'm heading.

I put in a functional day. I go to work, I go to the gym, I grocery shop, I watch a sitcom. The monotony creates this internal Batman, screaming for an adventure, wanting to live on the edge, wanting to fight crime and bust the villains. But the blatant desire turns me into the Joker. The glory of something-anything-is enough of a change from the picket-fenced, perfect life I'm living. It's a dangerous mix. And it's a very fine line between sanity and just completely losing my shit.

There are places where the people live in huts with dirt floors. They walk six miles with a bucket to collect sewage-tainted drinking water. I should be happy and respect what I have and the mediocre success I've attained. But fuck those third-world skinny kids. Fuck them. They need to break out. We are the same, with different circumstances. Fuck me. I need to break out. But neither of us do it. We are conditioned for acceptance, and we can bear more hardships than we think, all for the illusion of comfort.

It's not that I lack compassion. It's not that I feel like I live in some ivory tower. We are both victims, but we self-sabotage. We don't change because we think we can't. It's a universal tragedy. It is human. So that's why I drown it all out at the bottom of a bottle, it numbs out the feelings, the complacency. It kills the drive of ambition, the guilt of success and the lack of respect for that success. It allows me to forget that I'm not thankful for what I have, that I'm a terrible bastard. I'm dying for someone to wake me up, but I'm a very deep sleeper and the task seems nearly impossible.

# Hot Summers, Global Warming, Dead Babies

The heat index is 110. Swamp ass occurs if you think too hard. Walking outside is like stepping into a hot bath with your clothes on. You are wet. It's a mix of sweat and ambient humidity. You almost need scuba gear to breathe out there. I came home on my lunch break from work on Wednesday just to take a shower and change my clothes. This is ridiculous.

***The Global Warming Debate Is Heating Up***. It's a tongue-in-cheek headline to grab the attention of the idiots who need catchy headlines to care about shit. Someone over-thought how clever they were and it came off pretentious. It reads like a Mad Magazine headline. I don't subscribe to the magazine or the idea of global warming but damn this is a hot summer.

It rains at about one or two every day. The Floridian summers, they say. Par for the course, they say. You would think that the reprieve from the heat via the rain would be a welcome one. It's not. A wake of steam follows each fat raindrop. It hits your skin and burns you where it lands. It's not acid rain, it's just hot water but you still don't want to be out in it.

The thunderstorms are epic, too. Thick bolts of lightning, the split second blind spot marring your vision if you accidentally look directly at it, and the auditory assault of the accompanying thunder all wreak havoc on your senses. The raw sky is green, and threatens tornado touchdowns. The meteorologists talk about hot air mixing with cooler air to cause it. I actually scream bullshit at the TV. There's no cool air out there.

The massive downpours only cause to enhance the humidity afterwards. The ground is saturated. The earth can't suck up enough of the water to help it dissipate and so now you've got puddles all over the map. Retina-burning sunlight amidst large lakes of ground puddles. The puddles are tolerable, but the wet conditions and the standing water are breeding grounds for Mosquitos. Full grown, they attack you relentlessly. They are the size of pterodactyls and they are not afraid of humans. They've crossed the border from insect to big game. I have a few of their heads on wooden plaques in my library. Mowed them down with scatter shot. The only things I'm missing are a pair of khaki shorts, a safari hat, and a Jeep Wrangler with fog lights on top.

People leave their babies and their pets in the car and run into the store. They are surprised when they come back to find dead bodies. The protests fork in one of two directions every time. "I forgot I had a baby/pet in the car," or "It was only for a couple of minutes." Every time. They exist simultaneously. It's Schrödinger's Cat. Every summer the news feed gets clogged up with stories of morons who don't understand that this heat can kill. It's sad at first, but then you start to believe that the baby/pet never had a viable chance for survival in the first place. Not with some sort of custodial intervention. The baby/pet was doomed because she/it had dumb parents.

So anyway, that's this week's gripe. In a few months the suffocating, debilitating heat will be over and we'll just be back to normal annoying heat. It will be a welcome downgrade from living, as I currently do, on the surface of the sun.

# A Job Is A Job.

In true form to the category I have assigned my posts…"Dear Diary" seems most appropriate in this case….

So. Here's the deal. I have decided that the notion of disliking your job is ridiculous. Once upon a time, and not too long ago, I was all in on that idea. Jobs are terrible. Jobs are something we do while we earn the money to do the thing we fantasize about during the grind. Recently, though, I've realized two things.

**ONE.** My attitude about the job is a direct contributor to how I feel about it. So, maybe I clean toilets. If I go into it having a good attitude about cleaning the toilet, my emotional state about the job is positive. If I go into it thinking that it's disgusting and don't want to do it, the whole thing is negative. It's not the job that is good or bad, it's my attitude about the job.

**TWO.** Performance anxiety. Does my boss think I'm doing a good job? That's what I care about. If I know I'm doing a good job, it's not enough. I want my boss to know it. And more than that, I want to *know* my boss knows it. That creates anxiety and fuels my perception of dislike for a job. I don't like feeling that I have to constantly prove myself. I know I'm good. I'm good with my performance. I know I'm ethical, and I know I will always do my best. If a boss doesn't see that, should I care? What can I really do about it? I'm already firing on all cylinders, I can't increase productivity. I'm already doing my absolute best. Yes, is the answer. I *should* care, because if my boss doesn't believe I'm doing my best work, then ultimately I could get fired. But also, I should keep in mind that getting a pink slip doesn't mean death. I will survive. If I resign myself to simply doing my best and not worrying about the perceptions of someone else, my like for the job increases. Therefore, again, the job is the job. The anxiety to produce and the stress and pressure that anxiety creates is what I don't like. The job is fine.

The problem for me is my utter lack of confidence. Behind the cool and collected façade is a child, wishing desperately for validation. Hoping that the adult, the boss, will accept my performance as good. It is a deeply seeded desire to make "daddy" proud. It's inside me and I struggle to change it. Because of it, I'm destined to assign my dislike to the job rather than the real factors. I will never be happy with a job in that case because those issues will manifest themselves anywhere I decide to work. I change a job in hopes of changing those deeply seeded issues. I blame the job, but I need to look past that and cope with the real underlying issues.

# The Torment Of Memory

Bump up the volume on the radio. Outside, in the sun, with the breeze cutting the heat. Dogs bark in the distance, mixing with the sputter of lawn mowers a street away. The air smells like grass. It's reminiscent of years ago. If I really sit here quietly, I can recall everything. I remember kindergarten. The memories are random, connected only by these senses. I remember my fifth grade librarian. I remember. Everything. There's a sense of loss when I recall them. Sentimentality is sad. People say it's a happy sort of sad, but I think they're wrong. When you remember something and you know you can never get it back, there is an emptiness, a feeling of loss.

Bump up the volume. It's loud enough to drown out the concentration required to access the memories. The present often preoccupies me enough to push them out, to ignore them. They are back-burner material. It's the quiet times, a smell, a feeling that brings them up to the front. And most of the time I stifle those thoughts. It's too sad. School. The cafeteria. My first job, those days. I remember it all. It's overwhelming. It's colors and sounds and youth. The clatter of silverware brings me there, the transition from summer to fall, the air. All of it. I imagine that death comes when your mind simply can't hold it all in anymore. It's an accumulation. Plaque.

First love. Naïveté. First kisses. They have evolved into deformity. There is no longer a wide-eyed wonder. The butterflies flew away. Call it age, call it wisdom or call it desensitization. Call it whatever you want, but experience is overrated. I've seen it happen. The soft curves and clean lines of youth marred by age. Gravity pulls on you, deconstructs the life cycle. We trudge on toward the end. The thought of it coaxes the butterflies back. It's something new, something to experience with wonder again. Something…different.

So I bump up the music. It's an effort to push out those memories, those experiences, to wipe the hard drive clean, and to experience a "first" again. I long to misplace importance on something trivial again, like a child, because I don't know any better. But the music can't get loud enough, the alcohol can't flow eternal, and the hard drives that are my memories can't be restored to factory settings. They need to run their course. There is no new operating system to install over the clutter.

Bump it up, just a little more. Ironic that I might damage my ability to hear by the volume and then I'll be relegated to sit in silence with just the discordant memories of my youth, to confront the sadness even the happy ones cause. Bump it up, just a little bit louder, so my attention is monopolized by something that overpowers even the loudest memories...

# I Think I've Figured It Out.

In the prism of this pace, the light fractures at odd angles. I almost want to bash my brains out with a steel hammer, or one of those spiked hammers used to tenderize meat. It's frustrating. That's all I'm saying, so don't call the suicide watch on me just yet.

People. Wow. Some people. Everyone. The perception of speed is sticky. If you can't move fast enough, if you can't adjust yourself to happily integrate into the positive perceptions of others, you'll get stuck in that sticky mud for sure. It's one-thirty AM. The glow of my iPad creates a halo of ones and zeros on my face. Photons trip through the thick atmosphere and decay on my oily skin. It's the same glow people at the restaurant get stuck in, the same glow of light speed texts about nothing. College students. They are simple texts like 'k' or 'ttyl'…they are texts riddled with misspelled words disguised as abbreviations. There's two more letters in the word 'you' but this is life, baby. It's fast-paced. We don't have time for two more letters. They simply aren't efficient.

The gas pedal can't go any deeper into the floor board. Time can't stop. Gotta keep moving or the dust of the people zooming by will choke you. It's a Doppler nightmare. An auditory assault. Nature is overpowered by artificial sounds. Even when it's quiet, my ears still ring from it.

The speed of life, the rat race, the rush hour is now the rush twenty-four hours. The Earth can't sleep to heal, the parasitic infestation of humanity splits, quadruples, octuples….in a blink we could be cannibals In a blink, we have over-reproduced, overpopulated and the food supply lines choke out and we become our own food supply line. Baby fingers become the caviar of the rich, they're a delicacy. Tender. Perfect with a splash of Tabasco.

This blue and green oval populates exponentially and it will get tight in here.

But wait…there's still…

Space. The closed ecosystem of earth is suffocating. We move. We migrate. We are a bacteria. We colonize. It's manifest destiny into the stars. Suddenly there's maneuverability. Suddenly there's room for farms and crops and fields and cows again. The big question is whether or not we can get there before our population chokes itself out. So it's a race for the technology to accomplish it.

The infection of humanity will devour everything without concern for the future it will force us to live within. We are animals. We are selfish. We will survive. We will kill each other to survive. And that's why pace is important. That's why I need to be faster than the assholes around me. The last one there is the rotten egg. The last one there doesn't get there, because he's already dead. Make no mistake about it. It's a brutal competition dressed in the clothing of being a good sport.

There's pressure. And the pressure to speed up, to outpace those around us, and the unyielding constriction of overpopulation is ultimately why people sometimes flip the fuck out and napalm the DMV.

# Focus

Steam rises from my coffee cup. It gives the liquid inside it a sense of depth, a sense of character. I focus on it closely, blurring the objects further off into the distance behind it. It's like a photo taken with a big zoom, for macro pictures.

The quiet moments, the observational nuances, the early morning-alert-from-the-correct-amount-of-sleep vividness detonates creative explosives in my mind. I notice that when I'm tired, I can't produce. No amount of steamy coffee can fully open my eyes. The physical act is there, but the mental acuity is not. I'm on auto pilot for most of the week, going through a trained set of motions, getting through the day, and grinding it out. There are highlights. It's a set of sports-centeresque clips of great moments. I trash the unfavorable ones; they can't make the cut. I push them out as though they never existed and years from now, I'll only be able to recall the highlight reel. It is an acceptable arrangement.

Being alert is underrated. I'm not sure it's possible to pull it off 100% of the time. We are not designed that way. There is always going to be a level of zombie in our behavior, going through a standardized set of actions. It's the reason people don't see what is in front of them, or can't remember a face or a name. Our attention is not focused. We are off the mental grid. I read somewhere that streamlined focus creates joy in whatever task is taking place. Mood levels increase with focus. Not sure if it's true, just something I read.

Unfortunately, my head is in the clouds. I'm a dreamer. The grass is greener, blah, blah. But also I am mostly happy. In counterpoint to the article I read, my happiness stems from the dream, from the lack of focus. So I'm not sure if the article is wrong or if I'm just an anomaly. I almost wish it's the latter. In some small way, I'd like to think I'm different from the masses, that I blaze a trail off on my own.

I step over great roots, chop a path through the brush. The trail is not easy, but it's my own. Robert Frost wrote poems about this shit.

# My Writing Is Shit.

My writing is shit. It's okay, I've accepted it. Also, as a separate, debilitating blow, I am incapable of improving. I don't learn, I don't get better, I am a stagnant, non-learning, uncreative buffoon. The more I write, the shittier I get. It's the Midas touch in reverse. Golden treasures turn to shit when I inflict my gentle touch upon them.

I am inept, and sluggish. I lack originality. I lack basic fundamentals. I can't learn. I look up how to use a semicolon on a regular basis. I can't retain the knowledge. I am not a good writer. I am not a better writer than my peers. I am doomed to fail. I'm also too dumb to give up on it. Two publishers saw a spark in my writing enough to want to at least attempt to work with me, but I was blinded by ignorance and arrogance. Readers found my work incomprehensible. I vomited words on a page and thought it was decent. I read back through it and I hate it. It is sub-par writing.

The torment of a writer. The struggle. The self-loathing. The impossible task of getting paid for a creative work. It's a discouraging climb. I've climbed it. But I'm still in the foothills with not a single rope or carabiner. I have not packed my lunch. I do not even have hiking boots. I thought flip flops were a good idea. There is gravel and loose dirt. With every step I make toward a summit that I cannot see, I slide backwards in the gravel. I don't even know if there *is* a summit.

I've been on the verge of surrender. I am on the verge of surrender, but I'm stubborn and can't accept failure. Furthermore, I can't not write. It is who I am, it's in the fiber of my being. I am destined to put a tremendous amount of effort into my mediocrity. I will stay mediocre, since I'm incapable of improving. It is frustrating and glorious.

I will die into obscurity. No level of success will be mine. No one will know my name or read my works. I almost don't want them to. It is an embarrassing collection of failures. But I keep them published because it's all I have. I cling to a hope. I cling to impossibilities. The mental anguish and struggle of being accepted into a writing community that is already over saturated with terrible writers wears me down. They are denying my membership. I can't even get in *there*. I tell myself its okay. I persevere. I hate myself for persevering. I love hating myself.

So I continue…

# Keep Your Stupid Blue Ribbon

There's not a first place ribbon for being great at what you do. Fame, money, blah blah. I'll take it, but all I ever really want is a first place fucking ribbon. A little swatch of blue fabric that proclaims how great I am at something. One that says I'm the best. The douchebag next to me got that stupid red one. Second place. It's a marker for all to see that someone was better than him. That he got bested. Good try, but here's a reminder for you that you still suck.

But there's no ribbon. The boss isn't handing those out today, not ever. I might get a certificate that tells me I accomplished something, but it's not a blue, first place ribbon. I want other mother fuckers to know that they got bested. I want to pin it to my chest triumphantly and go on a tour. Point people out of a crowd and tell them they got beat. By me.

It can't happen though. There's no blue ribbon. Even if there were, I'd be the person in the crowd getting pointed out for how someone beat me. I don't work hard enough, fast enough, and I'm not smart enough. That's the point though, I guess, and why there's no blue ribbon to begin with. There's always someone better. Always. The problem isn't competition, the problem is the fourth dimension. Time. No one can hold onto greatness indefinitely. Blue ribbons should have a disclaimer: 1st Place, this time.

Somehow, despite knowing the limitations of greatness, I still believe there's a pinnacle, a plateau that I can reach where I will believe I have arrived. It's an illusion, a pipe dream, it simply doesn't exist. There will always be another hill to climb, I will never stop and say, well, I guess this is it, there's no better I can be.

We have to manifest this illusion of destination to motivate us to keep going. It's a parlor trick, a slight of hand, because otherwise we'd be too discouraged to even try. It's sort of disappointing, really, to think about. But also, it reminds me that there's not a ceiling. There is no best. There's no limit to the potential we possess. Not so discouraging as it is encouraging, and now the blue ribbon almost seems like a barricade, like someone telling me that there *is* a limit, and I get a little pissed off that there's this guy judging me and telling me its okay to stop reaching, that I'm the best.

So this guy can keep his ribbon. He can shove it right up his stupid ass. I'm going to keep reaching. Give that blue ribbon to the guy that wants to arrive, the guy that believes he should stop pushing for greatness. The blue ribbon is a stop sign that too many people obey. I want to blow through it with local law enforcement in hot pursuit. They can't stop me. I want to hit speeds unheard of. I want it to end in a terrible crash, so people will say that in that moment, in *that* particular snippet of time, I was the greatest there ever was.

# Gotta Write!

Here I am. The over-sized, ceramic coffee cup is still too small, but any bigger and the handle won't support its own weight. I blindly trust the structural integrity. The handle will not crack right off the side when I lift it and there will be no crotch burning this morning. Not from a lap full of scalding coffee, anyway.

Gotta write, gotta write, gotta write…I only have a few precious moments of creative Zen every day. Its right after I wake up, after a piping cup of coffee, but before the real meat of the day begins. There's a small window of glorious creativity. Sometimes it hits late, and I already thought the moment was over. I'm in traffic, at a stop light, and it floods into me like I took a limitless pill. I'm wound up and ideas click. I can almost hear the electrical synapses in my brain firing off like mini explosions. But I'm stuck. In traffic. The moment will pass before I can get my clumsy fingers to the keyboard.

I torture myself with this. I imagine myself crashing through the line of cars, steering wheel turned a near-ninety degrees, and pushing through into the emergency lane. Gotta write. I speed by the stagnant mass of vehicles jammed up on the morning commute. A car is using the emergency lane for its intended purpose, hood up, engine smoking. I swerve into the grass around it. Gotta write. Gotta write.

The incomplete off-ramp is a good place to make a jump if I can gain enough speed. I accelerate and barrel toward the missing section. The ramp up can't take me all the way across to the other side. The car is too heavy and it begins to plummet down. Gotta write. I roll down my window and jump out as the car descends into the last stages of the suicide leap.

I'm in open air now. I'd follow the car down to my death, but I'm able to rip off my belt and hook it over a low power line. I zip line to safety as my car explodes from the impact. It over-explodes, as though there were bombs strapped to it and were detonated on impact. Glass and chunks of metal hit the concrete around me, but this occurs in slow motion to make me look cool as fuck.

I get home, sit in front of my computer, but the moment has passed. I was close that time, but creativity cannot be forced. I have lost 48 cars this way. And 17 belts.

# Umm...what...? Yeah, I'm Losing It.

Staring at a blank page, aching to write something–anything, but not knowing where to start. It's a typical snapshot of my writing. I just start, without a direction most times and as I gain momentum, I end up bouncing up to some sort of cohesive idea. Sometimes I bounce too high and smack my head on the ceiling, but more often than not, I'm trying to get traction through quicksand.

So today I was slogging through the rainforest, but now I'm deeply mired in a muddy sinkhole. I can't move my legs. And since I travel alone, there's not even someone to throw me a rescue branch. I could die right here if I weren't so stubborn. I take turns in this swamp. Some days it's blogging quicksand, some days it's novel quicksand. Doubt creeps in...well, to be honest, doubt is always around. It doesn't even creep anymore, it sits on my shoulder and laughs at me with reckless abandon. What I'm describing here, however, is those times when it's not just laughing at me directly in my ear, it's also choking me. As I'm sinking in quicksand.

Someone asked me recently about a muse. If I had one, she abandoned me a long time ago. She was tired of getting taken for granted, probably. I got complacent. I had Han Solo arrogance. I was amazing. Then this. This quicksand of creativity, with doubt on my shoulder, a book in the bag, the pressure of a sophomore work looming over me like a cloud of poisonous gas. I breathe it in deeply, coughing, and knowing its killing me but I can't help but to inhale. I somehow think my lungs just automatically will know or adapt to reject it. How's that for irony? Doubtful and confident at the same time?

Anyway, just a thought before the rest of my life eats me alive and I become too senile and weak to carry on. That's something to look forward to, though. When senility finally breaches sanity, I bet I'll be a seriously good cackler. I will cackle so hard and with such reckless abandon, they'll want to use me for Halloween effects. Maybe then I'll reach the pinnacle, the top, where I'll have an assistant, whose sole purpose is to wipe the drool from this old man's chin. My assistants will have assistants. I won't have time for basic hygiene, I'll tell them. I have wicked witch-level cackling to do.

# Baby Advice?

Death begins at the moment of birth. It's a countdown. The clock is ticking, so you better start making something of your life. I tell this to all the babies I know. But they are arrogant and think they have all the time in the world. They think they have all the answers. But I'm old. I've lived it. It would do the arrogant babies some good to have a little respect for what I'm telling them. They don't have the ability to respond, the mental and muscular capacity to react, but that's okay. Just listen, baby:

- Get ahold of your emotions. You own them, they don't own you. Don't forget and get it reversed. There are adults that still haven't grasped this yet, so start practicing now. The adults may not cry like you do, but they do the equivalent. They don't even realize that the fit they're throwing is embarrassing them. Fucking morons. Sorry about the language, baby, you haven't learned that yet.
- Try new things. From new foods to physical challenges. Don't let the fear of failing in front of others keep you from trying. Try it. Take failures in stride because that's how you learn and grow. If you are never willing to try, you'll be just like every other boring asshole out there. Forgive the language again, but you need to hear this. Sugar-coating is for the millennials and you're beyond that. Struggle. It's a good building block to understanding and appreciating things.
- Save money. Spend money. There's a balance to it. Make money doing what you love and don't settle for something you hate because it's more comfortable than taking a risk on doing something that fulfills you.

That's it, baby. Spit out the pacifier, the binky, whatever you kids call that rubber nipple nowadays. It's impeding your ability to be taken seriously. Get a goddamned suit, and pull yourself together. Time's-a-wastin'.

# I Write...Weird Stuff That No One Understands.

Today I got the novel moving again. From stagnation to holy shit, what a bizarre plot twist. It has to connect. I went out in left field to connect it, at chapter twelve. 20,000 words deep, the spin pulls whole plots of land up along with it. The gravitational force is leg-breaking. I keep telling myself that's what first drafts are for...to work in all the shit you want, but know you'll end up cutting out in the end. Well, I rigged myself this time. The twist is so embedded into the plot, it's impossible to run away from. So I guess I'll just have to take a little extra care with it. Hold the exposition, push into the action. Keep a subtle hand, but shove it down some throats....we'll see how the agent likes it. We'll see how she forces me to reign it in, as if I'm even capable of reining anything in.

"This story writes itself. I'm sorry that it's boring. Wait for the 180 in chapter twelve," I'll say. "It'll blow your fucking socks off. But also, you'll find it stupid and unbelievable. Enjoy!"

But I work on commission, so I'll bastardize it however she tells me to, and that crazy turn will either become the whole story, or won't make it at all. It's fine. I'm a 'yes' man anyways. If I chose to be a 'no' man, I wouldn't get my royalty checks and that just cannot stand. I've only written two books in my actual name, with no secret alias–ahem–pen name. Two books that say, hey, look at me! I'm a person! I legitimately wrote only two books. The other ones, under different names, were mine too, but I was afraid of failure back then and didn't want the association. If they were successful, and you've heard of them, I'd never be able to convince you that I'm the one who authored them. They don't even bear my name. Doesn't matter either. Who cares who wrote them? The check bears my name, and I bought stuff because of it, so fuck you for not believing that I'm established. I'm putting that right at the top of my resume.

A flux capacitor could only bring me to an alternate past. One where I put my actual name on things I've put out there. It wouldn't really matter anyway. I'd still be in this house, same car, same beer in hand. I'd still be hallucinating-drunk and sloppy at life. That means I'm an artist, right? Inability to pull my shit together=creative fucking genius. I like that. It has a ring to it. Bill C. Castengera, creative fucking genius. If I ever make it big, I'll knight people with that title…I'll make them kneel ceremoniously and I'll pull out a different implement each time. "I christen thee a creative fucking genius." Tap the terribly done makeshift Harry Potter wand on each shoulder. "Now rise and create, you son of a bitch." People will watch the coverage worldwide. Daytime TV will be interrupted for it. That's how big it will be.

If I hit it that big, maybe the other books won't matter. Maybe the Pope attends the ceremony and I knight him too, for being a 'Badass for the Lord.' Eventually I'll just go on tours randomly creating shit to christen people for. Then I'll be outed as a fraud and die in shame. Maybe I'll get stoned to death like back in the old days. I don't even care. It was worth it and I don't regret any part of it.

# Muses Are Pre Madonnas

So…the weekend. It's coming up on 4 o'clock and all I've done today was watch a bunch of YouTube videos. All day. I'll wake up on Monday and iron my shirt, get ready for work, and wonder what happened to my weekend. I didn't work on the novel. I slogged through short stories and blogs in an attempt to de-clot the pulse. I can barely find it anymore. The pads can't shock me back either, it seems. Not today. The muse took a radical vacation. Maybe she quit and burned a bridge. Not even a two weeks' notice. I really thought she was more responsible than that. Damn these millennials. Where's her sense of responsibility?

So I'm on my own. That's fine. Her inspiration was garbage anyway and I can do that just fine on my own. Maybe I'll find an overqualified muse this go round. Guilt her into staying for at least a year. One that comes to fucking work on time. One that keeps the drama at home. I need a professional. A real go-getter. I'm not even being picky. Any one of the nine will do…

Yeah, so until then, I guess its YouTube and web surfing. I'll check the applicants in a few days and weed out the bad ones, the ones that don't have the decency to complete the personality profile or sign up for a professional looking email address, because "twisted_thong69@gmail.com" can never work in a professional environment. Email is free, FYI. Pull it together, muses. No 401k, either, not until she can do the work. But, let's spin that positively and suggest that she can say she's been with me before my meteoric rise to the top. Lock her in to a contract. That's the plan.

So if any of you know a Homerian-caliber Greek muse that needs some contract work, let me know. Maybe she can get me to flip that off switch on the Xbox…

# The Steampunk Mind

Sometimes I'm amazing. Sometimes things click right into place and there is this amazing sense of universal harmony. It's refreshing when that chain of events occurs, and I have the presence of mind to slow down and see it. But since the misery, these glimpses are rare. So for the most part I hate everyone and everything. I'm an absolute joy to be around. My only saving grace is that I'm quiet. I don't have much to say, the cogs and gears in my brain are ratcheted tightly down, whirring in perpetual motion, greased up in a beautiful steampunk package of bronze and copper.

Not a single piece of the intricate mechanism is attached to my mouth. The gears spin fast. My mind is a dynamo. My mouth is a special needs child, an autistic counterbalance to the natural genius of my thoughts. I'm verbally inarticulate, and I can't convert thoughts through the dam of my vocal cords. I answer people in one word sentences, I allow awkward silences, because I can't express my thoughts into tangible sounds. People probably get a sense that there's not a whole lot going on in my head. I seem simple.

Beneath that impression, though, I assure you, there are vast expanses of intelligent thoughts and emotions. My inability to dumb down to participate in small talk makes me appear one-dimensional. My wit is quick, a sharpened tool that moves faster than people expect. So fast, in fact that I arrive to a point several steps ahead of the current conversation and people are lost and confused by it. So I zip it up and shut down the voice box. The tin man is out of oil for his jaw line, and his lips are rusted shut. The elements and lack of use close any chance of restoration.

Look deeply into my blank eyes and you might see the gears through my open pupils. They are spinning so fast they look dead stopped and you'll probably think I'm not there, that my presence is a shell, with no guts or substance. And perception is reality. The truth is what is observable, and I'm starting to believe it. As my assimilation continues, my gears slow down, they conform to the standard and then I feel like a victim of society, a result of pop culture, self-loathing, and an insatiable desire to fit in with my peers. The spark dims, the wheels tire, and the oil can remains a barren cavity. The rust-cancer is infecting all moving parts, grinding them, eventually, to a halt. The powerhouse of thought and reflection normalizing to a status quo and the perception finally becomes the reality.

# I Don't Move, Baby

So, yeah, I'm a loner, baby. I like people. I just don't like the tangled mess they leave in their wakes. It's emotional garbage. Drama llama. That snare is deep, baby. Emotions are beautiful, and wonderful and scary. They twist us up and manifest physically. I can't deal with my own emotional drama so when I get trapped in the middle of someone else's, it's like a beautiful work of art. Like van Gogh. I mean, it's like if van Gogh shit blood onto a canvas and sawed his own tongue off and threw it on there, letting it stick, but the weight of it makes it slide down just a bit, all red and bubbly with saliva like the ocean's foam. You know, subtle.

So I back it up and let people cage fight with the other cage fighters. I'm Teflon. Slick, like ice, baby. I sway. The blows get close but none of them can land because I'm in a dance. Where the forward advances create my back steps. The ref can't even avoid blows like I can. I'm fluid, and invisible. I will not get sucked in to any of that drama llama, baby. I just won't play.

I am an isolationist, a lone star, the last coin in your pocket. If you can move me, you can move the whole fucking universe.

# The Future Of Technology: The Idea Guy

I'm off the beaten path. I'm socially awkward but fake a shiny polish that makes me feel sleazy and disingenuous. The system of neurons and synaptic sparks in my brain fail to follow any proper engineering model. Maybe they had the blue prints upside-down.

So recently, I've had this idea that I was meant for much more than what I am currently exhibiting. I'm performing below standard. I can't shake the feeling that I was supposed to change the world, to enrich it in some way with fresh ideas, a game-changing invention. Something Steve Jobs-esque. But that ship is rapidly sailing. I had an idea for how to levitate very large objects with sound by matching the sound output to the harmonic resonance of the object being moved. It was earth shattering. I bet that's how coral castle was constructed. But I failed to follow through.

I had an idea for a cellphone that could double as a wireless mouse. I even began the process of patenting the idea, but my idea was too similar to something that Sony had already patented and did nothing with.

I have this idea for Nano-paint, made up of tiny, organic, bio-luminescent molecules. Using a computer, one could tell the molecules to change into any color of the rainbow. The applications for this would be endless, from car color to fingernail color, but I lack the knowledge and understanding of how to research and develop the idea. I didn't apply myself in school to build the foundation I need to be able to produce it

I have this idea, deriving from electrochromic glass (smart glass) that turns from clear to opaque to block out the sun like window blinds but with the touch of a button. The tech already exists, but my idea was to make refrigerator doors from this stuff, so that you can push a button and see the contents of your fridge without ever opening the door.

I have ideas. Vast expanses of ideas that can't come to fruition because I lack the funding or the knowledge or, in most cases, both.

The ideas here are simply the tip of the iceberg. These are the things that roll around in my head. I have ideas like these *ad infinitum.* If something can be imagined, human ingenuity can make that imagined concept a reality. I believe that we are limitless in our capacity to imagine and create, we just have to figure out inventive ways to materialize the ideas into reality with innovation. I'm the idea man, the brilliant mind that will fade into obscurity because contrary to my desires, ideas mean nothing without the equivalent action to validate the worth of the idea.

I bet idea-people come and go all the time, geniuses, and we never hear about them because they don't have the relevant balance of idea and action and the means to make the action occur. How much wonderful knowledge and creativity is lost because of it? We'll never know. Three hundred years from now, when all of these things are a reality, society can look back on this blog, and call me the Davinci of my time, the forward thinking, inactive genius that dreamt of the future and created none of it.

## About The Author

Bill C. Castengera lives in Jacksonville, Florida, with his wife and three children. He maintains a personal blog and has authored several books. In the words of his good friend and mentor, "Castengera's ability to understand human nature is remarkable."